# Novels for Students, Volume 30

Project Editor: Sara Constantakis Rights Acquisition and Management: Leitha Etheridge-Sims, Sari Gordon, Aja Perales, Jhanay Williams Composition: Evi Abou-El-Seoud Manufacturing: Drew Kalasky

Imaging: John Watkins

Product Design: Pamela A. E. Galbreath, Jennifer Wahi Content Conversion: Katrina Coach Product Manager: Meggin Condino

For product information and technology assistance, contact us at **Gale Customer Support, 1-800-877-4253.**

For permission to use material from this text or product, submit all requests online at **www.cengage.com/permissions**.

Further permissions questions can be emailed to **permissionrequest@cengage.com** While every effort has been made to ensure the reliability of the information presented in this publication, Gale, a part of Cengage Learning, does not guarantee the accuracy of the data contained herein. Gale accepts no payment for listing; and inclusion in the publication of any organization, agency, institution, publication, service, or individual does not imply endorsement of the editors or publisher. Errors brought to the attention of the publisher and verified to the satisfaction of the publisher will be corrected in future editions.

*Gale*
27500 Drake Rd.
Farmington Hills, MI, 48331-3535

ISBN-13: 978-0-7876-8687-1
ISBN-10: 0-7876-8687-5
ISSN 1094-3552

This title is also available as an e-book.
ISBN-13: 978-1-4144-4946-3

ISBN-10: 1-4144-4946-1
Contact your Gale, a part of Cengage Learning sales
representative for ordering information.

Printed in the United States of America
1 2 3 4 5 6 7 13 12 11 10 09

# *Franny and Zooey*

## J. D. Salinger 1955-1957

## Introduction

J. D. Salinger's *Franny and Zooey* was first published as two separate stories in the *New Yorker*, with "Franny" appearing in the periodical in 1955 and "Zooey" appearing there in 1957. Though some critics might describe *Franny and Zooey* as two linked short stories, both episodes feature Franny Glass and both take place in almost immediate chronological order. Thus, the continuity of the two stories, as well as their connected and over-arching themes, legitimizes reading *Franny and Zooey* as a full-fledged novel. Indeed, they were published as such in 1961 and since then have been reviewed and discussed as a whole. *Franny and Zooey* has become an American classic; among Salinger's work, it is second only to his foremost classic novel, *The Catcher in the Rye*. Notably, both books have remained mainstays on high school curricula and reading lists for several decades.

*Franny and Zooey* is not only an examination of the Glass family but also a critique of materialism and New England intellectualism. First and foremost, it is an exploration of the intersection between art and spirituality. The book, remarkably, has remained in print since its initial publication. A recent edition was released in 2001 by Back Bay Books.

# Author Biography

J. D. Salinger was born Jerome David Salinger in New York City on January 1, 1919. His father, Sol Salinger, was a successful importer, and the family, including Salinger's mother, Miriam, and his older sister, Doris, enjoyed an upper-middle-class lifestyle. Salinger showed an interest in writing from a young age, neglecting his academic career in favor of this pursuit. He graduated from the Valley Forge Military Academy just outside Wayne, Pennsylvania, in 1936. He next attended New York University, where he wrote and pursued acting, for only one semester. He spent the following semester at Ursinus College in Collegeville, Pennsylvania, where he wrote for the school paper. He also briefly attended Columbia University. Salinger was drafted into the U.S. Army in April 1942. While stationed at Fort Dix in New Jersey, he completed the first draft of his best-known novel, *The Catcher in the Rye* (the book would not be published for another nine years). Next stationed overseas and trained in counterintelligence, Salinger saw action in the famed Battle of Normandy and also participated in the liberation of France. In 1945, he married a French doctor named Sylvia. Little is known about her or the marriage, and the couple divorced in 1947.

After being discharged from the army in 1945, Salinger turned down Simon & Schuster's offer to publish a collection of his short stories. He spent the next few years doing little more than socializing with other literary figures, most of whom congregated in the Greenwich Village neighborhood of Manhattan. When Salinger's first novel was finally published in 1951, it was met with immediate and widespread approbation. Salinger adamantly refused to step into the limelight as the book's author, refusing book tours and interviews and even going so far as to have his picture removed from the book's cover. Two years later, in 1953, Salinger moved to Cornish, New Hampshire. That same year, several of Salinger's short stories, previously published in periodicals, were collected and released as *Nine Stories*. The book was a brief bestseller and received good reviews, though it was not nearly as successful as *The Catcher in the Rye*. On February 17, 1955, Salinger married Claire Douglas, a student at Radcliffe. The marriage lasted for twelve years and produced two children, Margaret Ann and Matthew.

Salinger published two books during the 1960s, but the content of both publications was initially published in magazines during the 1950s. *Franny and Zooey* was released in book form in 1961, but it was first published as two separate stories in the *New Yorker*. "Franny" appeared in the periodical on January 29, 1955, and "Zooey" appeared there on May 4, 1957. *Raise High the Roof Beam, Carpenters; and Seymour: An Introduction* was published in book form in 1963. Like *Franny and Zooey*, the book consists of two lengthy short stories that were first published in the *New Yorker*. "Raise High the Roof Beam,

Carpenters" appeared in the periodical on November 19, 1955, while "Seymour" was printed there on June 6, 1959. Notably, both books feature characters from the fictional Glass family. Both books also became bestsellers, though their critical reception was lackluster.

On June 19, 1965, Salinger published "Hapworth 16, 1924" in the *New Yorker* (it was later released in book form in 1997). Though Salinger has reportedly continued to write, no new publications have been released since then. The author has continued to live a reclusive life, making every effort to avoid the public eye. When an unauthorized collection of Salinger's work, *The Complete Uncollected Stories of J. D. Salinger*, was released in 1974, Salinger stepped forward to denounce it. He stepped forward again in 1986, filing suit in an attempt to stop the publication of a biography about him. The biography, Ian Hamilton's *In Search of J. D. Salinger* was to include several of Salinger's unpublished letters. Ironically, though the biography was eventually published in 1988 without the letters, much of the contested correspondence was reprinted in newspaper articles that covered the initial court battle.

# Plot Summary

## *Franny*

It is a wintry Saturday morning and the big Yale game is to take place later that afternoon. Several male students are at the train station waiting for their girlfriends from the nearby women's colleges to arrive. Lane Coutell braves the cold and stands alone on the platform, rereading a letter from his girlfriend, Franny. In the letter, Franny sounds like a typical adoring girlfriend who loves and misses her boyfriend. It is clear that the letter is important to Lane. When the train arrives, Franny asks Lane if he received her letter, and he responds with feigned nonchalance. Lane asks Franny about the book she is holding, but she says it is nothing and puts it in her purse. She lies and tells Lane she missed him and guiltily holds his hand. It appears that Franny's letter was disingenuous.

The couple is eating lunch at Sickler's, an elite college hangout. Lane feels proud to have such a pretty girl with him. Franny notices his pride and feels guilty for noticing. Lane talks at length about a paper he wrote, though Franny seems distracted. She interrupts him to ask for his martini olive but feels bad when Lane looks affronted by the request. Though his hurt look has ruined the taste of the olive for her, she pretends to enjoy it. As Lane goes on about his paper, she accuses him of being a student who uses his brilliance to tear things apart (as opposed, supposedly, to building things up). The two squabble about this for a bit and order more martinis. Franny apologizes for her behavior and says she should have taken the semester off, that school is an "incredible farce." She apologizes again as Lane presents counterarguments against this statement. Lane will not let the matter drop, even as Franny apologizes yet again.

The two move into a discussion about what defines a true poet. Franny grows increasingly pale and repeatedly states that she does not feel well and does not want to talk about poetry. Lane persists until Franny excuses herself to go to the restroom, and then he finally begins to show concern for her well-being. After Franny has gone to the restroom, Lane sits alone at the table looking dejected. When he sees a fellow student at another table, Lane changes his expression to one of cool detachment.

---

# Media Adaptations

- An unauthorized film adaptation of *Franny and Zooey* was released as *Pari* in Iran in 1995. Through the threat of legal action, Salinger prevented the film's New York City debut during the 1998 Iranian Film Festival.

- The 2001 Wes Anderson film *The Royal Tenenbaums* features characters loosely based on the Glass family and contains some scenes reminiscent of those in *Franny and Zooey*. Written by Wes and Owen Anderson and released by American Empirical Pictures, the film starred Gene Hackman, Anjelica Huston, Ben Stiller, Gwyneth Paltrow, Luke Wilson, Owen Wilson, Bill Murray, and Danny Glover.

---

In the restroom, Franny enters a stall, sits on the floor, and holds herself as she sobs loudly for several minutes. She stops suddenly and removes her book from her purse. She hugs it, puts it away, washes her face, and then walks, smiling, back to the table. Lane asks Franny if she is all right, and Franny replies that she has never felt better. They order lunch, but even Franny's plain meal (she requests a chicken sandwich) annoys Lane. He tells her that they are meeting Wally Campbell at the game. Franny cannot remember meeting Lane's friend, though Lane says they have met several times. Franny replies that Wally looks and acts like everyone else and is thus eminently forgettable. She apologizes before Lane can chastise her, but he does anyway. Franny repeats yet again that she does not feel well, that she feels like she is going insane. Lane is concerned and asks if anything has happened. Franny says she is fine.

Franny tells Lane that she quit acting because it was too much about ego (hers and everyone else's). She explains that she does not want to be like everyone else, just trying to make a name for themselves. Franny repeats that she feels like she is going crazy. Lane asks Franny about her book for the second time that day, and Franny again tries to avoid the question, but Lane persists. Franny tells him that the anonymously authored book, *The Way of the Pilgrim*, is about a man who reads about ceaseless prayer in the Bible. The man sets out to learn how to do this and meets a sage who teaches him how to use the "Jesus Prayer": "Lord Jesus Christ, have mercy on me." Lane seems to be paying more attention to his food (frogs' legs and escargot) than to Franny. He mentions his paper again and ignores Franny's recommendation that he read the book.

Franny tells Lane that the secret to constant prayer, as it is laid out in the book, is that you first repeat the prayer over and over using your lips. Eventually, the prayer becomes second nature, syncopated with a person's very heartbeat. It is at this point, according to the book, that the petitioner experiences a new spiritual awakening. The constant prayer ultimately allows a person to see God. Franny is clearly enamored with the idea, citing similar and numerous examples to be found in vastly different religions and religious texts. Lane remains unimpressed. By now, Franny is chain smoking and has not touched her sandwich. Lane dismisses the idea of spiritual awakening as a psychological phenomenon. The waiter clears their plates. Lane tells Franny he loves her, and Franny responds by excusing herself to go to the restroom. On her way there, she faints by the bar.

Franny regains consciousness on the couch in the manager's office. She says she is embarrassed but otherwise fine. She is worried about missing the game, but Lane insists on taking her back to the girls' dormitory where she is staying for the weekend. Even in the midst of his genuine concern for Franny, Lane crudely hints that it has been far too long since they have been intimate. He goes to get them a cab, and Franny, now alone, begins to move her lips as if she is repeating a silent prayer.

## *Zooey*

Though the narrative up until this point has been in the third person, it now changes into the first person. In a roundabout way, the narrator indicates that he is Buddy Glass, writing in 1957 about events that took place in November 1955. After identifying himself and his family's objections to the way they are about to be portrayed, Buddy lapses from the first person to the third. Buddy describes his handsome little brother Zooey Glass. Zooey is twenty-five years old. He is soaking in the bathtub in the Glass family's Upper East Side Manhattan apartment, smoking and reading a four-year-old letter from Buddy. Zooey is a successful television actor and the second youngest of seven siblings, five boys and two girls. At this point, a footnote in the narrative names all of the Glass children in order of their birth. The eldest, Seymour, committed suicide in 1948 at the age of thirty-one; the second eldest, Buddy himself, is a writer in residence at a women's junior college in upstate New York. Buddy is followed by Boo Boo, a married mother of three. Next in birth order are the twins, Walt and Walker. Walt was killed in 1945 during the occupation of Japan, and Walker is a Roman Catholic priest. The twins were followed by Zooey. Following the footnote, the narrative returns to the main text with a mention of Franny, the baby of the family, eighteen years younger than Seymour. All of the precocious Glass children took part in a radio program called *It's a Wise Child*.

Buddy presents the letter Zooey is reading in its entirety. It was written on the three-year anniversary of Seymour's death. In it, Buddy writes about both the sadness and hilarity of traveling to Florida to retrieve Seymour's body. He also talks about how both he and Seymour were adults by the time Zooey and Franny were born, and how the elder brothers took it upon themselves to teach their youngest siblings everything they could about Eastern religion and philosophy. Buddy also talks about how he waited a year after Seymour's death before seeing Zooey and Franny, hoping to avoid the painful task of sharing in their grief. The letter is the first instance in which Buddy has broached the subject with either of them. Buddy next talks about Zooey's acting career in the letter, calling his little brother by his full name, Zachary Martin Glass. Buddy states that if Zooey ever does "anything at all beautiful on a stage, anything nameless and joy-making," then Buddy and his dead brother will visit Zooey backstage with flowers.

Zooey finishes reading the old and creased letter and then begins to read a script. His mother, Bessie, soon knocks on the door and asks to come in. Annoyed, Zooey puts the script down, draws the shower curtain, and invites her in. While Bessie is ostensibly entering to bring Zooey some new toothpaste, she really wants to know when he is going to talk to Franny, who has been camped out on the living room couch having a nervous breakdown for the past couple of days (ever since the big game at Yale). Zooey gives a noncommittal answer and asks Bessie to leave. Instead, Bessie sits down and says she does not know why Buddy insists on maintaining the private phone line that he and Seymour had in their old room, when Buddy does not even have a phone at his current address. (This complaint has been raging for over four years, as Buddy mentions it in his letter to Zooey.) Zooey says his mother is being stupid. She ignores him and keeps talking about the phone; she wants to get in touch with Buddy and tell him about Franny.

Zooey keeps asking Bessie to leave and she keeps ignoring him. She says that Les (Bessie's husband and the Glass children's father) is also concerned about Franny but that "he's never faced anything as long as I've known him." As if to prove her point, Bessie says that Les still listens to the radio in the vain hope that he will hear his children again (including Seymour and Walt). She says Les "lives entirely in the past." Indeed, Les's solution to Franny's emotional distress has been to offer her a tangerine. Zooey laughs. Bessie calls Franny an "overwrought little college girl that's been reading too many religious books." Like Lane and Franny, Bessie and Zooey have been intermittently bickering throughout their conversation. Both fall silent until Zooey threatens to get out of the tub whether his mother is in the room or not. Bessie leaves but says she will be back. She reminds Zooey to use the bath mat.

A few moments later, Zooey stands at the sink shaving. Bessie reenters the room. She returns to the topic of what should be done about Franny, and Zooey returns to his combative sarcasm. Bessie mentions that Lane has been calling and is concerned for Franny. Zooey says Lane is only concerned about how Franny feels about Lane, not how Franny feels in general. Bessie replies that Lane is the one who told her about Franny's religious book. Franny told Lane that she got the book from her college library, and Bessie says the library should not carry such texts. At this, Zooey becomes very upset. He tells her the book and its sequel, *The Pilgrim Continues His Way* (which

Franny has also been reading), were taken from Seymour's desk in the room he shared with Buddy. The books have been there since before Seymour's death, and Zooey is offended that Bessie did not realize this. Bessie sadly explains that she avoids going into that room. Zooey apologizes.

Several times throughout their conversation, Bessie has been comparing her male children with one another. Zooey finally gets fed up with this and tells his mother that Buddy tries to be like Seymour in so many ways that he might as well kill himself too. He also says that Buddy and Seymour turned him and Franny into "*freaks*" with their childhood indoctrination in Eastern belief systems. He tells Bessie that because of his brothers, he secretly says a prayer called "The Four Great Vows" before every meal, and that he has done so for the last fifteen years. The one time he tried to eat without saying the prayer, he nearly choked on his meal. Bessie has never even heard of the prayer. Zooey again asks his mother to leave the bathroom and she responds by saying that she wishes he would get married. Zooey laughs.

Zooey warns Bessie not to send Franny to a psychoanalyst. He reminds her of what psychoanalysis did for Seymour. He says it will drive Franny to an insane asylum or worse. He also outlines the content of the books that Franny has been reading. Bessie says this explains why Franny has been muttering to herself for the last few days. Zooey and Bessie soon begin bickering again, and Bessie again asks Zooey to talk to his sister. Zooey says he would if he had something useful to say. By now, he has finished shaving and is putting his shoes on. Bessie finally begins to leave the bathroom. As she does, she tells Zooey, "in the old radio days ... you all used to be so sweet and loving to each other it was a joy to see." She adds, "I don't know what good it is to know so much and be smart as whips and all if it doesn't make you happy."

Franny lies sleeping on the couch in the living room. The room is excessively furnished. It is also cluttered with the memorabilia from *It's a Wise Child* that Les has collected. Zooey, now fully dressed, wakes Franny, who tells him about a dream she was having. The family cat, Bloomberg, is lying with Franny. She and Zooey discuss Zooey's new scripts. During their conversation, Zooey notices that Franny's lips are moving. Zooey critiques his scripts, but when Franny asks why he works on projects he does not like, he says, "Because I'm tired as hell of getting up furious in the morning and going to bed furious at night." He says he hates himself because he makes people feel like they do not want to do good work, only work "that will be thought good." Franny says she is ashamed that this is exactly what she did to Lane. Zooey replies, "We're freaks ... [Buddy and Seymour] got us nice and early and made us into freaks with freakish standards ... and we're never going to have a minute's peace, the rest of our lives." Franny pets the cat and continues to move her lips throughout the conversation. Zooey says, "I could happily lie down and die sometimes."

Franny says she would tear her fellow students apart in the same way that Zooey has described, even though she would hate herself for doing it. She tells him she could stand college if there were any acknowledgment that knowledge leads to wisdom. She states that in nearly four years of attending college, the only time she ever heard the word "wise" was in reference to a retired politician who made his fortune in the stock market. She says that knowledge has become as much a commodity as all the other "treasures" people spend their time collecting. Zooey points out that Franny is trying to do the exact same thing with the Jesus Prayer, trying to amass something "that's every ... bit as negotiable as all those other more material things." He asks her, "Does the fact that it's a prayer make all the difference?" Zooey wonders if the difference for Franny is "in which side somebody lays up his treasure—this side or the other?"

Franny admits she's been asking herself this very question. She says it is this conundrum (not the prayer or college) that has led her to have a breakdown. Franny is crying. Zooey looks out the window and watches a little girl playing with her dog. He says, "There are nice things in this world ... we're all such morons to get so sidetracked." Franny continues to move her lips. Zooey tells her that he does not intend to dissuade her from her prayer. He admits he once thought of doing it himself. But, he also says that he doesn't like Franny's approach. Though she is clearly in pain, her behavior has also been hurtful to their parents, and Zooey disapproves. He adds that while he agrees with

Franny's dislike for the ego-infested academic world, she takes her dislike too far by making it personal. However, he admits that he is often guilty of the same thing, even though he knows better.

Lastly, Zooey tells Franny that when she was ten, she decided she no longer liked Jesus because she disagreed with his teachings, namely that man is superior to other animals. Based on this, he concludes that Franny is "constitutionally unable to love or understand any son of God who says a human being, *any* human being ... is more valuable to God than any soft, helpless Easter chick." He accuses Franny of saying the prayer to Jesus as she would like him to be, not as he was. Given this, he asks how the Jesus Prayer is going to help her. Zooey asserts that Franny's breakdown is being caused by faulty logic and that persisting in faulty logic will not make her feel any better. By now, Franny is sobbing uncontrollably. Zooey realizes that he has failed his sister. He wanders around the living room aimlessly and then apologizes. This only makes Franny cry louder, and Zooey leaves the room.

Zooey runs into Bessie in the hallway. She wants to know about his talk with Franny, but he waves her away and goes into his room. He comes out a minute later with a cigar in his mouth and a white handkerchief over his head. For the first time in seven years, he enters Seymour and Buddy's old room. Zooey closes the door behind him and begins to read the quotes posted behind the door. The quotes are taken from various religious texts, novels, and famous philosophers. Zooey then sits at Seymour's old desk for upwards of twenty minutes. He suddenly stirs, opens up one of the drawers, rifles though it, and half reads Seymour's notes about his twenty-first birthday party. Zooey puts everything back in the drawer and then sits for another thirty minutes. Afterwards, he goes over to Buddy's desk and picks up the phone. He removes the handkerchief from his head and places it over the phone's mouthpiece.

Franny and Bessie are in the living room when the phone rings. Bessie goes into her bedroom to answer it. She returns and tells Franny that Buddy is on the phone and wants to talk to her. She says he sounds like he has a cold, which Franny also notices when she gets to the phone. "Buddy" asks Franny how she's feeling and Franny starts to complain about Zooey. When "Buddy" makes a disparaging remark about Zooey, Franny realizes that she is actually on the phone with Zooey, not Buddy. Franny tells Zooey that she knows it is him, but Zooey persists in the ruse. He finally gives up and tells her that he does not really want to stop her from saying the Jesus Prayer. He does point out, though, that the prayer will mean nothing if she does not distance herself from desire. However, he says that Franny became a brilliant actress because of her earlier desire to do so. He says, "You can't just *walk out* on the results of your own hankerings …. The only thing you can do now, the only re*lig*ious thing you can do, is *act*. Act for God, if you want to." He also warns her about her previous criticisms of the audience and its ignorance. Zooey tells Franny that "an artist's only concern is to shoot for some kind of perfection, and *on his own terms*, not anyone else's. You have no right to think about those things."

Franny has not been crying during the phone conversation, though she has been silently holding her face in her hands. Zooey tells Franny about a time when he was scheduled to appear on *It's a Wise Child*. Although he did not want to shine his shoes for the radio show, Seymour told him to do it for the "Fat Lady." Franny says that Seymour once told her to be funny for the Fat Lady. Zooey then asserts that "*There isn't anyone out there who isn't Seymour's Fat Lady*." Everyone at school whom she despises, even her stupid audience, are all the Fat Lady. He says, "*Don't you know who the Fat Lady really is?* ... It's Christ Himself. Christ Himself, buddy." At these words, Franny can barely hold onto the phone because she is so happy. Franny and Zooey are both silent for a moment and then Zooey says that he can't talk any longer and hangs up the phone. Franny continues to hold the phone, listening intently to the ensuing dial tone. After a while, she puts the phone down, smiles contentedly, and falls asleep on her parents' bed.

## *Lane Coutell*

Lane Coutell is Franny's college boyfriend. He attends Yale and is a member of the intellectual and upper-middle-class elite. Lane is very conscious of social expectations and conforms to them religiously. For instance, though he loves Franny and the letter she wrote him, he responds to both with feigned nonchalance. Lane goes to great lengths not to appear vulnerable and to bolster his masculinity. He is also extremely upset by Franny's behavior while they are at Sickler's. While Lane orders such delicacies as frogs' legs and escargot, as would be expected of him in such a restaurant, Franny orders a plebeian chicken sandwich. Lane is barely able to hide his annoyance at her order, and he is even more annoyed when she leaves her meal untouched. Lane is acutely aware of other people's perceptions of him. When Franny goes to the restroom and Lane sits looking dejected, he immediately changes his expression to one of cool detachment when he sees a fellow student.

Lane's constant preoccupation with how he is perceived makes him insensitive to Franny's clearly distressed state. He barely listens to her and prefers to talk about himself, even as Franny repeats that she does not feel well and thinks she may be going insane. Though Lane's genuine concern for Franny does surface at times, Lane constantly undermines that concern with his own selfishness. Even after Franny has fainted and he is being truly accommodating to her, he hints that it has been a long time since they have been intimate. Lane is the embodiment of all that Franny is beginning to despise.

## *Bessie Glass*

The Glass family matriarch, Bessie is a former dancer who retains some of her former beauty. She is often to be found wearing a kimono-like housecoat with additional pockets sewn on around the Glass apartment. These pockets contain a plethora of odds and ends, as well as tools. All of the Glass children refer to her as Bessie and they often make fun of her. Buddy ridicules Bessie in his letter to Zooey, and Zooey calls her stupid in her presence on more than one occasion. Bessie has very strong opinions about her children and what is best for them; her abrasive approach to child rearing clearly upsets and annoys her children, as is the case when she barges in on Zooey in the bathroom and continuously pesters Franny to eat some chicken soup. Yet, it is also clear that Bessie loves her children and that she has their best interests at heart.

Bessie is more perceptive than her children give her credit for, as she calls Franny an "overwrought little college girl that's been reading too many religious books." She also makes a perceptive remark about Zooey's personality, one that gives him pause. Indeed, the narrator notes that Bessie is accustomed to making such statements and to the pregnant pauses they incite. Like all of the characters in the novel, Bessie constantly smokes. She is also largely responsible for the disarray and clutter of the Glass family home (she is almost a walking embodiment of that disarray). Bessie is also an archetype of maternal behavior; she alternately admonishes Zooey to use the bath mat, get married, and get a haircut.

## *Boo Boo Glass*

The eldest female child in the Glass clan, Boo Boo is only referred to by her nickname, and her full name is never revealed. Though she is described in Buddy's footnote as a married mother of three, little else is said about her.

## *Buddy Glass*

The second eldest of the Glass family children (and oldest surviving child), Buddy is a writer who is serving as writer in residence at an unnamed women's college in upstate New York. Buddy does not have a phone at his current residence, although he maintains the old private line that he and Seymour kept in their shared childhood room. Everyone in the family clearly looks up to Buddy and solicits his opinion. This is evidenced by Bessie's frustration at not being able to contact him during Franny's crisis, as well as by Zooey pretending to be Buddy on the phone (after his own attempts at consoling Franny have failed). The love and respect accorded to Buddy is also illustrated by the four-year-old letter from Buddy that Zooey has kept and continues to read. Bessie also compares Zooey to Buddy on several occasions.

Buddy's letter to Zooey reveals the pain of handling Seymour's suicide, as well as his acknowledgment that he avoided Franny and Zooey after the tragedy. He encourages his brother to act and act well (just as Zooey later does for Franny). Buddy also seems to be apologizing for his and Seymour's early influence on Zooey and Franny, for flooding them with so much Eastern philosophy, yet it seems that even this damaging behavior was well-intentioned.

## *Franny Glass*

Twenty-year-old Franny Glass is the central character of the novel, though not necessarily its protagonist. The youngest of the Glass children, Franny chain smokes her way through an emotional, spiritual, and intellectual crisis. At its core, the crisis itself is largely unremarkable (i.e., it is typical for someone her age). It centers around the unbridgeable differences between one's internal values and the external values celebrated in the world at large. What is remarkable, however, is that Franny struggles to cope with this crisis, and that she turns to the Jesus Prayer for consolation. Throughout her conversations with Lane and Zooey, Franny demonstrates that she dislikes the academic world, the commoditization of culture (making culture into a product to be bought and sold), and intellectual and spiritual conformity. She is also disgusted by the role that ego plays in all of these perceived ills. This is why she finds the theory and practice outlined in *The Way of the Pilgrim* and *The Pilgrim Continues His Way* so attractive. It is also significant that these books belonged to Seymour.

When Zooey argues with Franny about her behavior—that while her objections to academia are valid, she takes them too personally, and that the Jesus Prayer is invalid because her recognition and understanding of Jesus is insincere—Franny cries inconsolably. She also admits that the underlying reason behind her breakdown is not her distaste for the commoditization of culture but the question of whether or not her attraction to the Jesus Prayer is also a form of commoditization. Yet, in the end, it is Zooey's suggestion that Franny turn her acting into a form of prayer that begins to console her. When Zooey describes the Fat Lady as both a symbol for everyone, including the audience, and a symbol for Christ, he is conflating everyone (the audience) and Christ, indicating that they are one and the same. Through this argument Franny finally finds peace. Zooey has rationalized Franny's acting for her as a form of the Jesus Prayer itself.

## Les Glass

Les Glass never appears in the novel and is

only referred to a few times by Bessie and the narrator. A former vaudeville performer, Les is described as a man who does not face anything and who lives in the past, decorating his living room with memorabilia of the children's radio heyday and listening to the radio in the hopes of hearing his children (alive and dead) again. According to Bessie, Les impotently tries to console Franny by offering her a tangerine.

## *Seymour Glass*

Though Seymour has been dead for seven years, his figure (and his suicide) still looms large. Buddy's letter to Zooey is written on the three year anniversary of Seymour's death, and it is the first instance in which Buddy openly discusses the suicide with his younger sibling. Bessie's obliviousness to the fact the Franny has taken the religious books from Seymour's old desk is clearly upsetting to Zooey, though he relents when Bessie sadly admits that she tries to avoid Seymour's old room. Zooey avoids the room himself. He enters it for the first time since Seymour's death in order to use the phone to call Franny. That Buddy maintains the old phone in their childhood bedroom is also a clear indication that Buddy is not entirely willing to let go of his brother. Seymour's influence on Franny and Zooey in the form of his and Buddy's instillment of Eastern values is also clearly felt. Zooey and Franny both struggle not to tear down the art and people around them, a fact that Zooey attributes to this indoctrination. Seymour's suicide and the pain it has caused are further underscored by the military death of another Glass sibling, Walt. Indeed, Walt's life and death are barely remarked upon.

## *Waker Glass*

*See* Walker Glass

## *Walker Glass*

Walker is the fifth Glass child, born just after his twin, Walt. A Roman Catholic priest currently on a mission outside the country, Walker is affectionately referred to by his family as Waker.

## *Walt Glass*

The fourth Glass child and Walker's elder twin, Walt served in the military and was killed in 1945 in a freak explosion while stationed in occupied Japan.

## *Zachary Martin Glass*

*See* Zooey Glass

## *Zooey Glass*

Zooey can be considered the novel's protagonist, because although the action in *Franny and Zooey* revolves around Franny and her breakdown, it is Zooey's thoughts and ideas that make up much of the narrative. Zooey, like his mother and sister, is often smoking, though he prefers cigars to cigarettes. Five years older than Franny, Zooey shares many of her views, though he is far more equivocal about them. At one time he, too, considered saying the Jesus Prayer. Because of the similar world views that Zooey and Franny share, Zooey, of all the Glass children, is best suited to approach Franny. This is not acknowledged by the rest of the family, however, as Bessie tries to get in touch with Buddy in the hopes that he can help her. Even Zooey acknowledges this perception by pretending to be Buddy when talking to Franny on the phone. Nevertheless, although Buddy is narrating the events, he is not an active participant in them, and it is ultimately Zooey who assuages Franny's crisis. Because he has shared her feelings and learned to cope with them, he is able to impart all that he has learned to this effect. Notably, Zooey blames Buddy and Seymour for turning him and Franny into "freaks." He says that they "got us nice and early and made us into freaks with freakish standards ... and we're never going to have a minute's peace, the rest of our lives."

Furthermore, it is clear that Zooey has given much thought to the purpose of the Jesus Prayer, and to the nature of Jesus Christ. He is the person who takes issue with Franny's softening of Jesus to suit her needs. He says that Jesus is not as lovable as Saint Francis of Assisi, the champion of animals, but that he is the only person in the Bible who truly understood man's relationship to God. He assures her that the Jesus Prayer is meant to give the supplicant "Christ-Consciousness." These arguments lay the foundation for Zooey's statement that the figurative Fat Lady they perform for is both everyone and Christ. This latter statement is the balm that finally affords Franny some relief. It is the realization that inside everyone she despises, something holy resides nevertheless.

# Themes

## *Family Dynamics*

The Glass family dynamics in *Franny and Zooey* largely inform the characters' interactions. Zooey's and Franny's position as the youngest of seven siblings bonds them in a singular way. It explains why Zooey is the only sibling still living at home and why Franny would choose to return there when she can longer stand being away at school. That both look up to their older sibling Buddy is also clear. Zooey keeps and reads an old letter from his brother, and Franny is willing to speak to him on the phone even in the midst of her crisis. Yet, Zooey blames both Buddy and Seymour for his and Franny's unhappiness. Notably, Zooey and Franny are both on the verge of adulthood in a family where their older siblings have moved away to pursue their own lives and careers. Though Walt was killed in the military in 1945, it is Seymour's 1948 suicide that looms large in all of the family members' lives. Both Bessie and Zooey avoid Seymour's old room, and Buddy waits three years before broaching the subject of Seymour's death with Zooey. Franny's pilgrim books, which sparked her breakdown, were taken from Seymour's old desk. The Glass family matriarch and patriarch also shed much light on the family relationships. Where Bessie is nosy, bossy, and overbearing, Les is just the opposite. Bessie barges in on her children in the bathtub and dispenses unwanted advice. Les never faces anything and surrounds himself with memorabilia from the past, even hoping to hear his dead children's voices on a long-canceled radio show. This large sprawling family is filled with ghosts, literal and metaphorical, and it is this backdrop that sets the tone for the book's centerpiece: Franny and Zooey's philosophical discussions.

## *Critique of Intellectual and Cultural Conformity*

While Franny and Lane eat lunch at Sickler's, she criticizes Lane for conforming to the expectations of the intellectual elite. To Franny, the critical paper that Lane is so proud of is emblematic of everything that is wrong with academia. Instead of fostering a genuine pursuit of knowledge, college has become a place of intellectual one-up manship. A similar critique is espoused by Zooey when he says that the scripts he is working on, no matter how good they may be, are little more than commodities. In the first chapter of the novel, Lane is acutely aware of conforming to the expectations of those around him, he pretends not to care about Franny as much as he does, to look cool in the restaurant, and to order the right food there. Even the restaurant itself was chosen for its cultural cachet. Franny is also aware of the cultural stereotypes and roles that surround her. When she meets Lane at the train station, she matches the women around her to their various colleges, and she does so based on little more than their clothing and bearing. Even the train station, the big game, and the restaurant trip are all part of a larger cultural ritual in which Franny and Lane take part.

Later, when Franny tells Zooey that the acquisition of knowledge is akin to any of the other forms of materialism that drive society, Zooey points out that the Jesus Prayer is also a form of acquisition. The only difference is that Franny seeks to amass "treasure" in the spiritual world as opposed to the physical or material world. Franny admits that it is this realization that is behind her breakdown. Thus, amidst Franny and Zooey's critiques of the society around them, both struggle to find a means of navigating that society in a blameless way. In other words, both siblings must be able to live in a world they find fault with but without finding fault with their own methods for doing so.

# Topics for Further Study

- Do you think Franny or Zooey is the novel's protagonist? Can it be both? Write an essay in which you support your thesis, making sure to include examples from the book.

- Read another of Salinger's stories about the Glass children. Give an oral presentation in which you outline how that story affects your understanding of *Franny and Zooey*.

- Conduct a research project on Eastern philosophy and religion and share your findings with the class in a multimedia presentation. What aspects of your research can be seen in the novel?

- Write a third-person narrative about your own family. What family dynamics are revealed in your story?

---

## *Clash between Art and Spirituality*

This conundrum leads both Zooey and Franny to question how they can create art in a spiritually corrupt world. Both Zooey and Franny struggle with the ego inherent in making art. Since both are actors, both must also cope with the multiple egos inherent in communal art: the conflicting egos of fellow actors, script writers, and directors all trying to make a name for themselves. Then, of course, there is the ever-present audience (whom Franny views as inferior and ignorant). Yet both Zooey and Franny hate themselves for believing, and for making others believe, that they don't "really want to do any good work" but only want to make work "that will be thought good." Zooey explains to Franny that he keeps acting simply because he is "tired as hell of getting up furious in the morning and going to bed furious at night." Indeed, Zooey likely persists because of Buddy's letter. In it, Buddy encourages Zooey to act and tells him that were he to do "anything at all beautiful on a stage, anything nameless and joy-making," then Buddy and his dead brother would appear to greet him with flowers. The letter's importance to Zooey as both a brother and an actor is clear not only in the letter's worn and oft-read appearance but also in the fact that Zooey reads it before beginning to read a new script.

Though Zooey does not paraphrase Buddy when he convinces Franny to act again, he is clearly channeling his brother's advice when he tells her that "the only re*lig*ious thing you can do, is *act*. Act for God, if you want to." Just as Buddy wishes for Zooey to achieve something "nameless and joy-making," Zooey tells Franny that "an artist's only concern is to shoot for some kind of perfection, and *on his own terms*, not anyone else's." Thus, both siblings ultimately find that rather than allowing their art to conflict with their spirituality, they not only can work together but can become one and the same thing. This idea is further underscored by Zooey's conflation of the symbolic Fat Lady into a representation of both everyone and Christ. Thus, the audience they despise is transformed into Christ, and their art is no longer a wasted effort presented to the ignorant masses but instead a gift to Christ, a performance for Christ alone.

## *Diction*

Though diction simply means word choice, it becomes more notable when that word choice is stylized or idiosyncratic, as is the case in *Franny and Zooey*. Part of this is due to the fact that much of the book is composed of philosophical, intellectual, or spiritual discourse. Thus, the diction takes on a more instructing, elevated, or pedantic tone, as opposed to a conversational tone. The language of Freudian psychoanalysis (i.e., words such as *ego*, *superego*, and *subconscious*) is also used fairly often. Franny's frequent use of the term *ego*—in Freudian terms, a part of the human consciousness—is one such example. Interestingly, while the Glass family members are educated and highly intelligent, they often lapse into slang or ungrammatical speech.

## *Point of View*

The first chapter and most of the second chapter of *Franny and Zooey* is told from the omniscient third-person point of view, that is, by a narrator who is not a specific character in the story, is able to portray the thoughts of all the characters, or is otherwise all-seeing and all-knowing. However, the beginning of the second chapter is narrated in the first person by Buddy Glass. The first person point of view is often told by a specific character participating in the story or by a narrator speaking as "I," who is therefore unable to know the thoughts of the other characters or have knowledge of action taking place outside their immediate experience. Buddy states that both Bessie and Franny object to how they are to be portrayed in his version of the following events. He also states that the year is 1957, though he is writing about events taking place in 1955. This jarring interruption in the narrative causes the reader to question who was narrating the first chapter. It also causes the reader to question the factual nature of the second chapter. Indeed, though Buddy fades into the background by switching back into an omniscient third-person narration, the fact remains that Buddy is the person relating the story. However, he takes no active part in the events as they unfold. Thus, the reader must conclude that Buddy is relating secondhand information and wonder how accurate, therefore, it can it be.

# Compare & Contrast

- **1950s:** Many secular colleges are for either men or women only, and even coeducational ("coed") colleges have strict policies regarding single-sex dormitories. Curfews are also part of college life, and students who are not in their dorms by curfew risk suspension or expulsion. This is why, in *Franny and Zooey*, a train arrives full of girls who are meeting their boyfriends and why Franny is staying in a girls' rooming house during her visit.

**Today:** Far more secular colleges are coed, and many of those that are place few restrictions on dormitory life. Many dorms are also coed. Cohabiting couples are not subject to expulsion (as they were in the 1950s), and curfews are rare.

- **1950s:** Psychoanalysis, a school of psychology developed by Sigmund Freud, is gaining in popularity. It is also gaining respect and validity in intellectual, academic, and health care communities.

  **Today:** While psychoanalysis is still used by some psychologists and psychiatrists, it is not held in such high esteem as it once was. Several alternative therapies exist and are often more widely used. Psychiatric drugs and cognitive therapy are two such alternatives.

- **1950s:** The American culture of commodity emerges in the 1950s. America, finally at peace after two world wars, experiences the height of economic prosperity. This prosperity leads to the rise of the middle class and its purchasing power. This in turn spurs the commoditization of culture, a trend that both Zooey and Franny lament. Much literature written during the time also laments this tendency.

**Today:** While there is more awareness of the benefits and detriments of consumer culture, it continues largely unabated. In fact, much of the American economy relies upon consumer culture.

## *Conformity and Consumer Culture in the 1950s*

Following the economic depression that paralyzed the United States during the 1930s, relief was brought about by the military-industrial complex and American involvement in World War II. By the war's end, the United States was well on its way to economic prosperity, which reached its peak in the 1950s. The rise of the middle class at this time was largely caused by this economic boom. Also, by the 1950s, the widespread popularity of television perpetuated cultural images in an unprecedented manner. This prosperity was also behind the growing college culture, as more and more families could afford to send their children to college. Thus, the combined factors of economic prosperity, widely available standardized education, and the constant broadcast of cultural images led to a culture largely based upon consumption and conformity. This is the culture that Franny and Zooey lament; they find themselves unable to happily take on the yoke of mindless materialism. It is why Franny cannot stand the hollow academic culture that surrounds her; she finds that knowledge itself has been reduced to just another commodity—a means to an end, that of securing a good job. Indeed, for many people this was the point of attending college during the 1950s. In such a culture, the novel suggests, people become as unremarkable and interchangeable as the prefabricated homes and other standardized factory goods that dominated the 1950s. For instance, Franny cannot remember meeting Lane's friend Wally; he looks and acts like everyone else and is thus eminently forgettable. Salinger's novel is an overt critique of the conformity and consumer culture of the 1950s.

# *Influence of Eastern Philosophy and Spirituality*

Eastern philosophy and spirituality gained increasing popularity in the United States during the 1950s. This was partly because the exchange of information became more widespread because of the increased availability of television, film, and other media, as well as through academia. Yet the more likely (and compelling) reason behind the rising popularity of Eastern belief and practice in the 1950s is that its basic tenets were entirely antithetical to those espoused in mainstream American culture at the time. One such tenet is that material things are not only worthless but are no more than an illusion. Thus, it is impossible to place any spiritual or emotional value on belongings that are deemed inherently valueless. The Eastern religion of Buddhism, in particular, teaches its followers that desire kills the soul, especially the desire for material goods. All of these teachings and values are reflected in the novel (though Zooey blames his and Franny's early immersion in Eastern thought for turning them into "freaks"). Notably, Eastern thought and spirituality were reflected in much of the literature produced during the 1950s. The Beat movement (a 1950s literary movement) particularly emulated Eastern philosophy and spirituality, just as it lamented the consumer culture.

# Critical Overview

Though *Franny and Zooey* was an immediate bestseller, it received an ambivalent critical reception at best. Indeed, while most critics found the novel to be well written and well constructed, they ultimately took issue with the book's primary message, that everyone is Christ. For instance, *New Statesman* contributor Frank Kermode points out that "if it seems strange to be saying a Jesus prayer to a lot of louts in a theater, [Franny] is to remember that they're all Christ." Kermode goes on to remark that "it is to make us accept this conclusion that Salinger has worked so deviously. And, as one of his admiring audience, I find it hard to believe he could be selling anything so simple and untrue." Joan Didion, writing in the *National Review* states that "however brilliantly rendered (and it is), however hauntingly right in the rhythm of its dialogue (and it is), *Franny and Zooey* is finally spurious, and what makes it spurious is Salinger's tendency to flatter the essential triviality within each of his readers, his predilection for giving instructions for living." Emphasizing her point, Didion goes on to call the novel a "self-help [book] … for the upper middle classes."

In a rare positive review printed in the *Canadian Forum*, Hilda Kirkwood applauds Salinger's "artfully deliberate accumulation of detail," adding that the "writing is unique and justly celebrated." Contrary to most critics, Kirkwood notes that "one finds oneself in considerable awe of J. D. Salinger's power to transmit so eloquently the mood of the modern intellectual dilemma and to transmute it into such intensely moving stories as *Franny and Zooey*." However, regardless of critical opinion, *Franny and Zooey* has remained in print for over forty years, and the novel is a mainstay in school curricula. Though some may take issue with the book's spiritual message, few argue that the book is entirely without value. *Franny and Zooey* remains an important work by an essential American author.

## What Do I Read Next?

- J. D. Salinger's *The Catcher in the Rye* (1951) is his best-known work to date; the book launched Salinger to international fame and remains an American classic to this day. The story is similar to *Franny and*

*Zooey*: both books feature young protagonists who come of age through their struggle to accept the distasteful world around them.

- Lawrence Ferlinghetti's 1958 book of poetry, *A Coney Island of the Mind*, shares many of the themes of *Franny and Zooey*. The collection is also a definitive work of Beat literature.

- *Eastern Philosophy: The Greatest Thinkers and Sages from Ancient to Modern Times* (2006), by Kevin Burns, is an introduction to Eastern thought for the nonspecialist. The book is likely to shed additional light on any reading of *Franny and Zooey*.

- Another Salinger work essential to a deeper understanding of *Franny and Zooey* is the short story collection *Raise High the Roof Beam, Carpenters; and Seymour: An Introduction* (1963). The stories largely pertain to Seymour Glass, further illuminating the Glass family saga.

# Sources

Alexander, Paul, *Salinger: A Biography*, Renaissance Books, 2000.

Bode, Carl, Review of *Franny and Zooey*, in *Wisconsin Studies in Contemporary Literature*, Winter 1962, pp. 65-71.

Bryan, James E., "J. D. Salinger: The Fat Lady and the Chicken Sandwich," in *College English*, December 1961, pp. 226-29.

Didion, Joan, "Finally (Fashionably) Spurious," in *National Review*, November 18, 1961, pp. 341-42.

Ennis, Lisa A., "Salinger, J(erome) D(avid)," in *The Scribner Encyclopedia of American Lives Thematic Series: The 1960s*, Charles Scribner's Sons, 2003.

Horowitz, Daniel, *Anxieties of Affluence: Critiques of American Consumer Culture, 1939-1979*, University of Massachusetts Press, 2005.

Kermode, Frank, "One Hand Clapping," in *New Statesman*, June 8, 1962, pp. 831-32.

Kirkwood, Hilda, Review of *Franny and Zooey*, in *Canadian Forum*, November,1961, pp. 189-90.

Morgan, Diane, *The Best Guide to Eastern Philosophy and Religion*, St. Martin's Griffin, 2001.

Old meadow, Harry, *Journeys East: 20th Century Western Encounters with Eastern Religious Traditions*, World Wisdom, 2004.

Salinger, J. D., *Franny and Zooey*, Little, Brown, 1961.

Young, William H., and Nancy K. Young, *The 1950s: American Popular Culture through History*, Greenwood Press, 2004.

# Further Reading

Anderson, Sherwood, *Winesburg, Ohio*, Signet Classics, 2005.

> First published in 1919, this classic book of linked short stories is a portrait of a semirural town in middle America. Although not as central as it is in *Franny and Zooey*, a similar assertion, that everyone is Christ, is made in the collection.

Charters, Anne, *The Portable Beat Reader*, Penguin Classics, 2003.

> This compilation of Beat literature is a comprehensive introduction to an important American literary movement. Although Salinger was not a Beat writer, his work was composed at the same time and espouses nearly identical themes and values.

Marling, Karal Ann, *As Seen on TV: The Visual Culture of Everyday Life in the 1950s*, Harvard University Press, 1998.

> This collection of text and images attempts to document the advent of broadcast television, a phenomenon that defined the 1950s as the decade that forever altered American

culture.

Salinger, Margaret A., *Dream Catcher: A Memoir*, Washington Square Press, 2001.

> This memoir by Salinger's daughter offers a rare glimpse into the reclusive author's life, as well as his tenuous relationship with his children.

CPSIA information can be obtained
at www.ICGtesting.com
Printed in the USA
BVHW032219290622
641005BV00010B/302